TREMORS

GARY BECK

This publication is a creative work protected in full by all applicable copyright laws, as well as by misappropriation, trade secret, unfair competition, and other applicable laws. No part of this book may be reproduced or transmitted in any manner without written permission from Winter Goose Publishing, except in the case of brief quotations embodied in critical articles or reviews. All rights reserved.

Winter Goose Publishing
45 Lafayette Road #114
North Hampton, NH 03862

www.wintergoosepublishing.com
Contact Information: info@wintergoosepublishing.com

Tremors

COPYRIGHT © 2017 by Gary Beck

ISBN: 978-1-941058-64-0
First Edition, March 2017

Cover Design by Winter Goose Publishing
Typsetting by Odyssey Publishing

Published in the United States of America

"Je connais gens de toutes sortes
Ils n'égalent pas leurs destins
Indécis comme feuilles mortes"

—Guillaume Apollinaire, "Marizibill"

CONTENTS

Entropy	1
From the Terrace	3
Decline	4
Evolution	5
Middle Class Poets	6
To My Daughter	7
The Republic	8
Past Sighting	9
Crumbling Road	10
Sacrifice	11
Mild Protest	12
Pretty Picture	13
Futilism	14
Calculations	15
Free Will?	16
Errata	17
Loss	18
Commerce	19
Mass Destruction	20
Observatory	21
Dementia	22
Ailment	23
Ingrate	24
Sino Status	25
Trapped	26
Rejections	27
Shuttle Vision	28
Tempus	29
Surrender	30

One Season	31
Summons	32
Question	33
Lust Song	34
Inspiration	35
Faith	36
Tyranny	37
Ensnared	38
Emily Dickinson	39
Detached	40
Commuter Line	41
Duty	42
28th Year	43
Spring Song	44
Bus Trip	45
Decoy	46
Advice to Ex-Presidents	47
Travelers	48
Urban Spring	49
Fugit	50
Woman	51
Once Upon . . .	52
Mallorca	53
Relief	54
Auden	55
Eternal Struggle	56
Two Images	57
Shock of Recog . . .	58
Exodus	59
Hitchhiking North	60
Glib Adages	61
Disorder	62
Passion	63

Dwindling	64
Chance Meeting	65
Arrival	66
Last Gasp	67
Adult Education,	68
Another Land	69
Ode to Comfort	70
Off Course	71
Passivity	72
Purpose	73
Youthful Song	74
Portrait	75
The Poet	76
Transit	77
Glimmer	78
I Am 28	79
Burden	80
The Way of the World	81
Feeble Entente	82
Escapism	83
Exertions	84
Weary	85
The 20th Century	86
Flare-Up	87
Physics	88
Bound	89
Uplift	90
Inamorata	91
Seduced	92
Inertia	93
Helen	94
Strife	95
Flashback	96

Devourer	97
Concern	98
Love's Arrival	99
Sate	100
Profile of Failure	101
Striving	102
Weak Species	103
Migration	104
Joined	105
It Costs Ten Cents to Pee	106
Couch Potato	107
Coda	108
About the Author	110

The nature of poetry has evolved since the innovation of free verse and now should allow vast latitude of expression. Too many self-appointed guardians of the realm of poetry presume to righteously define the boundaries valid for exploration, arbitrarily excluding what may not appeal to their particular sensibilities. When some of the French Symbolist poets, in particular Rimbaud, Mallarmé, Apollonaire, and Valery, shattered the forms used for centuries and created free verse, resistance was automatic from the academics who scorned them. Those poets are venerated today as a vital part of literature.

The last major disturbance in the tranquility of poetry was caused by the Beats, who were dismissed as ill-disciplined, ill-mannered, disreputable advocates of sex, drugs, and rock and roll. Now they occupy a respected niche in the cathedral of poetry, having survived alienation from the mainstream despite excursions in autonomous verse, or unrevised stream of consciousness ramblings. Their contribution exploded some of the restrictions on style and content, but their accomplishments have become stratified, while their disruption of incipient ossification has been forgotten. They are now as tame as Byron, Keats, and Shelly, other forbearers who lifted the torch of rebellion against arbitrary constrictions on subject matter.

> Excerpt from "Raw Realism, a Poetry Manifesto,"
> by Gary Beck.

Published by Gently Read Literature, July, 2009

In memory of Don Peterson, a gifted playwright, with a keen mind that grasped the inequities and injustices in the world, a good friend

ENTROPY

When I was young
time seemed to pass
tortoise slow
agonizing me
trapped in school confines,
sterile rooms,
draining the spirit
from anyone
not facile.

Time speeded up
as I grew up,
though it took a while
for me to notice
and Albert Einstein
further confused me,
relatively speaking,
with theories requiring math
beyond my entropy.

As I grew older
time passed faster,
school days waiting for the bell,
decaying memories.
Vacations whizzed by
before I could enjoy them
and hardly refreshed
rushed back to burdens.

As old age creeps closer
brief time flees faster
and I am uncertain
that I can still accomplish
anything meaningful
in remaining days.

FROM THE TERRACE

After thousands of years
of uncomfortable evolution
I sit on concrete balcony,
far removed from nomad hordes,
earlier agricultural enclaves,
medieval conjoinings,
warming myself
in the weak spring sun,
not entirely different
than an elderly lizard
hulking on a heating rock
lethargically awaiting
the encroaching desert.

DECLINE

The world has grown smaller
since the information age
captured the human stage.
My world has grown larger
because of all the places
that I will not see
due to my infirmity.

EVOLUTION

I try to sleep
but cannot rest,
consumed by nuclear dreams,
mushrooming
through my fiery brain,
a reminder
of civilization
gone entirely mad.

MIDDLE CLASS POETS

A tolerant democracy
allows self-full, bloated poets
to hide in a university
sneering at the workings of the world,
secure in the protective cloak of tenure.
Once poets' voices raised the call
for freedom, other great causes.
Now most wallow in comforts
mumbling impotent objections
to current events
beyond their comprehension.

TO MY DAUGHTER

Star child
dreamful daughter,
uncrowned princess
of my regal thoughts,
you are the succession
of my highest aspirations,
not as imperfect as I,
somehow made better,
despite the lack of
bio-engineering.

THE REPUBLIC

This brief historical moment
may see proud endeavors pass
if we are forced to reject
the instant of democracy,
an immature belief
that shouldn't be lost
too soon, too soon.

PAST SIGHTING

Last night as I lay sleeping
I dreamed the roll call of the dead.
This was not Odysseus' descent
to the anguish of the underworld.
No Tiresias advised me of my fate.
I saw a processional of faces,
loved ones I have known and lost,
float in and out of consciousness
in mysterious dream-imagery.
The visitors had no admonitions,
prophecies, messages, requests,
just a ghostly presence
that for a strange interlude
restored lost memories.
When I awakened
I could not preserve
precious remembrance.

CRUMBLING ROAD

From coast to coast,
border to border,
the weeds poke holes
in your brief macadam coat,
speed limit sign 75 MPH
fallen on its face.
No one remains
to issue warnings
dangerous curves ahead.

SACRIFICE

I know the children of man,
blind-spilled on the earth
are born to waste,
devoured in crueler seas
by schools of predators,
feeding the bellies of Moloch heirs,
allocated to destruction
in the unprotected birthplace
of pitiless selection,
color, creed, credit card.

MILD PROTEST

Usually I spend my time
pondering the vast sweep of history.
War, man's greatest endeavor,
takes the bulk of speculation.
Science should come next,
but I was ill-educated
and settled for liberal arts.
International affairs now command
less attention then domestic affairs,
as my struggling society devolves.
So in a rare moment
of literary indulgence
I mused of petty changes
forced upon my poems.
I no longer dream of the Persian Gulf,
tainted by oil spills and Harpoon missiles.
I abandoned a renaissance address,
usurped by a pop culture Madonna.
I renounced the romance of the Nile
often flooded by ethnic cleansing.
Although these are trivial concerns,
undefended ivory towers
are fatally undermined
by harmful transgressions.

PRETTY PICTURE

Tonight's remembrance is pleasing,
a dawn discovery of three mama deer
with rambunctious, cavorting fawns,
the swimming hole at the brook,
the sudden afternoon torrent,
rain ending the jaunty day,
then the unexpected rainbow
and the squirrel of evening,
perched on dead sunset limb,
jabbering of sleep to come.

FUTILISM

Castles are only safe
from marauders
when built on hilltops,
their privacy maintained
by daily exercise
of oppressive power
harshly inflicted
on diverse vassals.

CALCULATIONS

Subtract from your highest value
the sum of all your disaffections
and there's not much left.
However you reckon,
you gotta have addition.
Most of us spent years
learning arithmetic,
though some of us
didn't take to it kindly.
But sooner or later,
even counting on fingers
results in calculations
that leave dissatisfaction.

FREE WILL?

The lines of destiny
in my troubled life
have never been as thin
as crossing, or not crossing
the next street,
turning the next corner,
expecting discoveries.

ERRATA

I fondle old mistakes
like precious jewels,
naked of setting,
cut and gleaming
in contracting hands,
shedding flakes of skin
in sweaty drops
rolled together
by impatient fingers
that twitch crystal flickers
for one moment's birth,
then blooded, die.

LOSS

I see too many faces
smileless masks
of drab routine,
bitter and shriveled
by diminished expectations.
They take no pleasure
in available gifts,
virtuosi robin's song,
a subtle burst of clematis,
elegant cloud formation.
Their hopes have been curdled
by too much desire
for material things.

COMMERCE

I cannot leave you,
yet untasted
whose bones, flesh cover,
proffer perfumed breasts
reaching for my hands.
Your beckoning loins
pronouncements of desire,
mine for the taking,
merely in exchange
for soft touch,
winning smile.

MASS DESTRUCTION

A pale, molecular vision
possesses me
and will not go away.
I am tormented
by chemical apparitions
seeking to consume
targets of opportunity,
terminating existence.

OBSERVATORY

My eyes wooed
the telescopic lens,
licking the least particles
of finite observation.
Its white so pure,
pocked by long craters,
bound by soft shadows,
made me think
this was no moon
I had seen before.
I paused in momentary awe,
(looked at a thousand nights)
now beheld between gasps.
Poets once sang of the moon.
Dreamers named their love the moon.
On this night one quarter gleamed
I saw a raw jewel's glow
birthing new vision
in my limited horizon.

DEMENTIA

The madman looks
in his fixated way,
with one eye at himself
and the other
at whatever
he can perceive.

AILMENT

My frail limbs,
sounded by physician's fingers
as if for auction block
are now defenseless.
My helpless body throbs,
the questing hands pull and squeeze,
while I lie in orbit of remoteness,
become another stranger,
hoping to endure.

INGRATE

Praise to the love of woman
that I forget in careless days
spent in spasms of creation.
Women who have loved me,
kind or cruel,
a moment or longer,
with bodies, thoughts,
sometimes something greater,
for any reason, so many ways,
never getting more than fragments
of my begrudging self,
I am fortunate to admire
such generous gifts.

SINO STATUS

U.S. relations with China
certainly seem to be fina,
despite recent confrontations
with nuclear connotations.
The leadership of Hu and Wen
brought them respect in the U.N.,
but still couldn't dissipate their mood
when sushi outsold Chinese food.

TRAPPED

How to avert madness
the schizoid cries,
trapped in the confines
of his fluttering head.
His search for sanity
is only postponed
by sheltering drugs,
hollow words,
professional regrets.

REJECTIONS

Often entrances are denied
to someone's warmth where we can hide
and pass the furtive, speeding hours
in their arms of sheltering bowers.
We dread the feeling of aloneness,
that conspires against togetherness.
So much waste concocting vagrant dreams
wearing the panic looks of shabby schemes
that fall from the weight of corrosion
without that instant of explosion
that buries all responsibility
beneath the shame of its own debris.

SHUTTLE VISION

The slow moon
made an angry rise,
while astronomers fretted,
a serpent of foreboding,
that the Hubble telescope,
its generous celestial eye
uncannily utile,
might be allowed
to casually drift off
in the cosmos.

TEMPUS

Time's indifferent hands,
intent on strangulation,
grip me day to day,
boding illness,
birthing dread,
resolving nothing
but nervous anticipations.

SURRENDER

The world is a spectacle
of material possessions
and sooner or later
most succumb to temptations,
appetites whetted by offerings,
power, pleasure, persuasions,
each manipulation
another acceptance
of shared corruption.

ONE SEASON

The winds of spring
come coyly kissing
with serpent's fangs,
bright honed and hissing.
Dripping venom
the tongue's songfest
falls on bleached sand
sterile, spent, at rest,
like a bold grey fox
of desert shyness,
who escapes his fate
because of slyness.

SUMMONS

My day of reckoning advances,
while defeat waits, and writhes and dances,
delighting in prospects of failure
that will ultimately bring closure
to dreams of poems that will not perish
as long as we seek truth to cherish.

QUESTION

Shall I go unsinging to my grave,
littering the callous wayside
with a childlike lament?
I would chant rivers, mountains, people,
soar far above the atmosphere,
if I could only learn to conquer
my betrayal tongue.

LUST SONG

Can I sing
that I covet your body,
with a tender lust of power,
dreaming you perfect,
wanting to rip into you
my imaginable longings.
My eyes of desire
creep your soft thigh,
tiny insects of June nights
hoping to feed their hunger
on the swell of round flesh,
gathered near your belly
until sated
I drift off.

INSPIRATION

Hail, poet. Praise for reawakenings.
For days in wasteful slumber spent
a kind, forgiving eye is bent
in some grandiose devotion,
playing the stops of absolution,
urging: seek your knee, penitent,
remember your unworthiness
has often led you to the doom,
the horror of a lonely room,
where fearful of oblivion
you squandered your brief span,
time's brief flirtation,
followed by desertion.

FAITH

"Ah brothers,"
the religious scholar said,
"in my studies I once read
of plagues of eld
and how they swept the earth.
My studies did not tell
of displaced souls
and the agonies they felt
not finding consolation."

TYRANNY

Time will our expectations crush
with casual disdain
and in our thoughtless failure rush
we cry defeat and wane.
We should oppression's hand defy
and scorn its blows and mock its curse
and with everlasting faith rely
that justice will our fears disperse.

ENSNARED

My hunger, my consumption
of too naked appetites
to be readily filled,
must starve with constant yearning
from eyes that would devour the universe,
to sate a bottomless belly.
Strangers too easily
pierce my isolated state
and mirroring entrapment,
refuse recognition,
leaving me prisoner
of my heedless self.

EMILY DICKINSON

Emily Dickinson didn't deplore
the frequent use of the metaphor.
She thought it better than to be
the victim of a simile.
So struggling poets who aspire
to set the literary world afire,
should seek their own mode of conjugation
and avoid Emily's subjugation.

DETACHED

Your rain of anger beats at me,
opening floodgates of destruction.
I lie beside your tremors,
silent, hoping to endure.
You accidentally shift
on purpose.
Your soft back
touches my unmoving hand.
I am tempted to pet your belly
and kiss away the splash of tears,
but I lie there withdrawn,
dreaming of tropic isles.

COMMUTER LINE

On Norwalk, Connecticut streets
the shabby people walk
and often stop to gawk
as the speeding train retreats.
The stares from each
are craving pity
from those who reach
the fabled city.

DUTY

Among soft women, soul,
I know you long to stay,
pausing in the penury
of each hesitation day.
Your bedroom much too often
is a cradle of retreat,
where you cower childlike
from the burdens you should meet.

28TH YEAR

This dream year
quickly fades away
without a sign of passing,
like a watermark
on the eroding sand,
leaving no trace
in the subsuming tide.
My visions have turned to denial,
my hopes to sad regret,
only my brief time remains
for my purer self of hunger
to build empires of fulfillment.

SPRING SONG

This day of joy,
my hot sun dreams,
many motions,
licking with yellowed fingers
the faces I hunger.
The strangers that pass
look with soft eyes
and tired mouths
as they woo shop windows,
laugh with their children,
walk mirage pavements,
while city streets sing:
spring, spring.

BUS TRIP

Whether it be hours,
or extended minutes
passing like Chinese torture,
I can not tell
encased in cross country bus
racing through darkness
to undesired destination
made distasteful by imagination,
anticipating arrival.

DECOY

I woo the queen of desolation,
her maddening breasts
two enticing mounds
filling my hands
with lustful expectations,
but crushing my hope
when crinkled tips subside,
rejecting my ardor
for alternate diversion.

ADVICE TO EX-PRESIDENTS

Do not mourn the passing of power,
for like other old men
you may still desire to be needed,
but stripped of sword and trappings
you can do little more
then seek an eclipsing dignity
that follows public service,
except for occasional summons
to ceremonious events.

TRAVELERS

Hitchhiking along the lost road
to fabled California,
but in reality nowhere bound,
watched by cacti, decrepit Indians,
we cross the enervating desert,
then the iced despair of mountains,
obstacles surely intended
to humble nouveau arrivistes.

URBAN SPRING

The park is bursting
with all kindsa things,
people, dogs, birds,
kids swinging like mad
on playground apparatus.
Look. There go two squirrels,
faster than heck.
I hope he catches her.

FUGIT

I would rather not submit myself
to less than my desire,
aspiring beyond accomplishments,
yearning for more than I can be,
while compromise seems surrender
and only time will determine
the degree of acceptance
of unforgiving fate.

WOMAN

I can do without you no longer
for I am an unfilled vessel
listening to the echo
of hollow plaints.
I yearn for your hands
that swell me to bursting
and know you do not fear
the hurt of penetration.
I have been unused too long
and detest my dust coat,
a throttling garment.
I would know splendid rainments
and transformed by your caresses
welcome the satiety of peace.

ONCE UPON...

Before time began to tell
insecure toilers to make haste,
the daily course of life
was ordered, simple, clear.
Sleep, rise, eat, fear, die.
The pangs of art,
or philosophy,
were not suffered long,
for the inexorable drudge,
survival, demanded all.

MALLORCA

I. First seen in the distance, from the air
a vision of brown, green mountains there,
as they stood a thousand years before
aircraft brought the tourists to your shore.

II. Largest of the Balearics, Queen
of Mediterranean specks, made green
through man's untiring persuasions,
despite conquests and invasions.
Romans, Vandals, Byzantine Empire,
Arabs, Aragon, they all expire.

III. I shall never forget the mountains
behind Valdemossa, rising into clouds,
with only the glint of a weather station
shining in the sun of modernity.

IV. Driving up the mountain road
where row on row the olives grow
and suddenly, between the terraced cliffs,
the sight of Soller,
crotched between tall mountains,
whispering of the sea, the sea.

RELIEF

An act of kindness spreads
ripples from a stone
breaking a still pool,
a determined assault
softening the struggle
that tests city dwellers.

AUDEN

W.H. Auden
generally never
writes without trying
to be terribly clever.
Some poets say things
whether little or much,
but Auden's too artsy,
with a posturing touch
like an old, cranky fogey
whose inarticulate curse
makes readers give thanks
that it could have been worse.

ETERNAL STRUGGLE

Our dream of world peace,
a bright expectation,
cleaves the dark blockade
of endless oppression,
reality our weakness.
The blood of visions
flows for no limitations
as the princes of power
tyrant our world.
The singers of struggle
pulse new passions
in the flame of unsurrender
and in the flare of hope
a bursting star appears,
our white-heat lover,
poeting the arrival
of tranquility.

TWO IMAGES

I   Parks are lonely
    when it rains
    forcing children
    to play elsewhere.

II Firemen should read Sartre
    before sliding down
    the long, cold pole.

SHOCK OF RECOG...

To woo without passion can't be compared
to explorations without ambitions.
But woman is a discovery,
her entrances a rare delight
to the worthy visitor.
To cross oceans, mountains, deserts
is not so far a journey, stranger,
as the distances in the newness of touch.
To want without hunger is an icy judgment
that must swiftly thaw, or freeze submerged parts,
no part hidden enough to avoid the lash
of self-awareness to pose, fraud, other sisters
of deceit, tumbling together like aging acrobats
combining clumsiness with straining smiles,
concealing panting breath, ugly recognition.

EXODUS

The torrid heat of the city,
drives the sweltering homeless
from the sweating parks.
They walk the condo'd streets
of prosperity,
like ancient nightmares
seeking sleepers to torment.

HITCHHIKING NORTH

They left me at a crossroads
and turned their jammed-crammed
station wagon full of kiddies
to seek a rest stop.
I stepped off the road to piss,
heard a stream, followed a sound,
found a fantasy pool,
clear, clean, icy cool,
waiting for a naked swimmer.
I plunged into renewal,
Blue Jay screamed: Thief. Thief,
although I stole nothing.
Afterwards, dressed, still shivering,
I walked the road, new born,
from water's pure deliverance.

GLIB ADAGES

Doubt and derision
distracts from decisions.

Blind faith and yearning
are worse than school learning.

Facile words in profusion
always lead to confusion.

Our claim to self-perception
is just one more deception.

DISORDER

Tormented thinker
of bombs and curses
hidden in your teapot
on the grimy shelf
of gingerbread psychosis
are tears enough
to start the world anew
(Were Noah drunk enough
to build again).
If your contention
does not deceive
each passing man,
there should be a way
to bring you peace,
before your dissolution
spreads its rage
in a bloody bath
on the unprepared world.

PASSION

Among our reasons for desire
we should admit infirmity,
since there are almost lifetimes
between quiverings of lust
and spasms of attainment.
Yet love has few enchantments
when we look its parts too closely
and may not survive inspection
without constant concessions.

DWINDLING

Forgetting is indiscriminate
obliterating what it pleases,
regardless of preferences
for information preservation.
Names, words, places, purpose,
all are vulnerable
to the scythe of dysfunction,
playing no favorites,
departing data at will.

CHANCE MEETING

Perhaps a woman is more tomorrows
than imagination can incline to,
rarely presenting new horizons,
but sweetening yesterday's visions,
until once again encounter time
bitters the mouth with loathing
and there is the unvoiced,
ever so gentle stirring,
of hope's shriveled corpse
that this chance meeting
of unperjured desire
birthing for woman a hunger,
will not vanish
doomed by self-despite,
but accord itself existence
and so us pleasure.

ARRIVAL

I listen to the evening bells
chiming the passing of hours
and look from my window of visions
at the ghost-haunted church towers.
I see nothing else save my own self,
rising like an almost Gibbous moon
announcing to the sleeping city
that my birth will be arriving soon.

LAST GASP

The hot sun licks my face,
an affectionate cat
pressing endearments,
but I stir no longer,
an old man
searching redemption,
envying younger men
awaiting desires.
When the remaining fruits
sour and shrivel
in my grasping hands,
I have no one left to implore
with my paltry shreds of hunger,
abandoned by time's judgment.

ADULT EDUCATION,

The inevitable tedium,
inescapable it seems,
carrying me into the past,
the same academic horror,
spending my soul sitting
in a sterile chamber,
listening to dreary talk
that painfully reveals
the student's vacuity,
the teacher's indifference,
the waste of passion.
Two nights each week
I crumble my desire,
my lust for learning
in this dullest of classes,
Expiation 101.

ANOTHER LAND

From my evening window,
night sounds, house lights,
are no different than in my land,
where I'm still a stranger,
adrift with expectations,
fevered with a passionate unreason
to possess someplace to call my own,
before I am defeated by imaginings.
I don't understand the language
and stumble through new words,
an infant on rubbery legs,
movement to new places.
Nevertheless, little is foreign.
Signs, speech, little things,
not the total bewilderment
of a child sprang into newness.

ODE TO COMFORT

Old poems of love
help us erase hate
and make us dream
sweet moods, noble thoughts.
New visions of torment
stab the heart,
penetrate deeply,
break off, fester,
leaving us marooned,
spiritually naked.

OFF COURSE

The myths of life
do not reveal directions
to endure the intolerable.
Each day's affront
multiplies its insolence
and the fool folds his hands,
nods his head,
submerges into dreams
upon a deathly bed,
intent on banishment
for a dire offense,
moral abstinence.

PASSIVITY

Some of us yearn for concealment. Some contain themselves in false endeavors, or idle creations. Almost all of us have nothing but the expectation of extinction, which poisons our tomorrows. We ply the illusions of destruction with passions. But those of us who perceive, yet do not act, who do not transmute ourselves into motion, bind ourselves to fixed orbits, and are denied the swirl of existence.

PURPOSE

Hallowed by my song,
not by words
spilling from unworthy mouth,
but the blooded moments
visioned by eyes
torn from desire to duty,
torrenting small resolves,
the gloried hungers of self
falling back unemptied,
still full of purpose,
but each defeat a glimmer
of destiny's infinite contempt.

YOUTHFUL SONG

This my twenty-sixth spring
and today I notice
what often in the past
I only gradually saw,
but this year,
led by new found power,
I sing of spring
and vision greatness.

PORTRAIT

America is wheels
spinning, turning, racing,
consuming man time
in futile searching
for lost destinations.
We rush onto our roads
urgently bound for somewhere,
are briefly serviced,
then pass on.

THE POET

Carried by unknown power
rapid past career and future,
the poet stirs from day to day
(sometimes not for months),
feeling his blind way,
senseless and forgetful,
often cruel and callous,
prince of dreamers,
singers,
failures.

TRANSIT

The morning subway of Brooklyn,
the distant chirping of sparrows,
the shiny rails, the rusted rails,
the city pigeons cooing
underneath the platform's eaves,
fighting, mating,
the sad brown rocks
beneath the tracks
absorbing commuter thrusts,
a timeless house
etched upon the blueing sky,
the squalid station
green-shingled and dirty
in the sun's neat eye.
A stranger walks on the platform
interrupting pigeon rites,
until the roaring train arrives
and carries off expectations.

GLIMMER

Never having overmuch resistance
to temptation,
how easy to submit
to blandishments
that offer the allure
imagined in heat of visitation.
So tempt me not to surrenders,
how often have I pleaded,
desire my undoing,
despite aspiring
to redemption.

I AM 28

The world's material promise
suddenly can fulfill
my desire for possessions
and stature in men's eyes,
but my poet self
resists the urge
to sacrifice myself
and wear ambition's coat,
possibly constructing
resurrection.

BURDEN

Gravity weighs me down
pressing on my bones.
What a strain to stand erect
with loss of efficiency,
endurance, energy,
leaving me willow frail,
bent or broken in every wind,
forced to wear clumsy coats
for shifting climes
and never escaping
planetary boundaries.

THE WAY OF THE WORLD

The ache of lust
for fortune's promise
births betrayal
into the kindless world,
rendering us slavethings,
peeking at life's treasure
with the hurt eyes
of deceived children.

FEEBLE ENTENTE

Events sometimes,
despite our fervent wish,
are not at our command
and all our desperate hope,
or proud determination
will often crumble,
leaving us fearful whiners,
not reconciled to fate.

ESCAPISM

Within my mind's imagining
are worlds of me that I invent.
I forget dreamlike visitations
when songless, selfless wonderings
submit their own realities
as substitutes for desire,
confining me, a passenger
on a vessel of delusion.

EXERTIONS

My own betrayal thoughts
prevent a place of honor,
a brief repose
for too much time spent
preparing failures.
I birth too little glory,
too much defeat,
dreaming of trumpets.
I would be worthier,
but subtract each day
from my living addition,
numbers beyond my puny calculations,
jeering with pinkest, bitter mouths
at unsuccessful ventures
of moral improvement.

WEARY

Because a little older now
I do not anguish less
the absence of a woman's kiss,
or ineluctable caress.
I long to lay my head
in desperate need of rest
for some time of comfort,
upon her sheltering breast.

THE 20TH CENTURY

The most inventive century
saw man achieve many wonders.
We heard his voice
from a thousand miles away.
He left the ground a moment,
then built swift machines that left the earth.
His science poured forth in abundance,
but we saw his fearful talents
turn hands to destructive war.
The killing art has many devotees
and we have seen too many wars
within our brief time span
that raised and felled nations, empires.
When the boots begin to march again
will we remember earlier devastation?
Have we found consolation
in aftermath construction?
The builders of horror are stirring
and certainly will not rest
until they possess us, or perish.

FLARE-UP

Desire annuls desire
when too desperate,
turning unremitting appetites
into clashing conjoinings
driving mad lovers
to suicide themselves,
consumed by excess hunger.

PHYSICS

So much then
of this careless youth
spent in fleeting moments
that are briefly lent
to use with care, or thrift
and then the swift decline
in which we fall
blazing bits of matter
churning the vast universe
for an instant of combustion
then dispersed into primal gas.

BOUND

My songless tongue
that utters its despair
for days that pass
without a moment's care
for things too brief
not destined to endure
that just breed grief
imprisoned by allure.

UPLIFT

Throughout my youth
I could not find
an outstretched hand
to nurture me,
but then I grew,
became a poet of power,
extended my hand
to nourish others
and sought redemption.

INAMORATA

I remembered your fragility
responding to an unkind word,
a thoughtless moment.
When last my fingers,
gripped hard to your flesh,
squeezed until my tremors burst,
the rising body under me soared
and moaned explosions.
After-breath and palpitations,
you against me
wet, soft, whimpering,
as my hand swam
in little pools
along your downed back.
Then a many-ended warp unraveled,
built with patience,
your unprotected self,
delicate as your pale nakedness.

SEDUCED

This infinite lassitude,
drowsed by your limbs
spilling over me,
a wave of newborn heat
quelling any feeble hope
of prolonged resistance.

INERTIA

Imponderable visions
hiding in my soul,
the soft underbelly
of aspiration
consoling itself,
through days of waste,
strangling from sleepless nights.
The slow, dormant rage
consuming my ambition
dulls the bright sword
that would cleave the world,
since I never forget this fleeting life,
spent as a dreamy prince
upon a sterile bed.

HELEN

Your mouth
a harbor of passion
invited my entry,
I the wrecker of cities,
the bearer of corpses,
fell within your sateless flesh,
birthed a voyage
and unleashed disaster.

STRIFE

Your sorrow
has never been
my pleasure.
The nights of torment
scarring our passion,
came from my self-hatred,
your unraveling greed,
so there was no resolution,
except pain, then departure.

FLASHBACK

A forgotten face from the past
suddenly emerged
from caverns of memory,
a brief, pained remembrance
of an obliterated episode
of madness, passion, loss.
Remote in my indifference
I watched it appear,
framed for a moment
in a dense, hurrying crowd,
then swept away without a word,
myself unwilling to seek omens.

DEVOURER

Your relentless love
that knows neither hunger
nor forgiveness,
has faded me,
a plant needing to be rooted.
You splurged my passion,
a careless child
playing hookey from feelings,
until at last,
I, the senseless sleeper awakened
and fled your putrefaction.

CONCERN

Another city night
birthing summer chaos,
as Venus hangs above the tenements
strutting her halo
before worried Hispanic eyes
watching their precious children
at play on squalid streets,
uncertain of their place
in the tenuous future.

LOVE'S ARRIVAL

Do not say
that love comes
a mad race,
roaring through the blood,
when it has quiet feet
padding in darkness,
a stalking cat's
stealthy approach,
that need not destroy
when brief desire
consumes hope,
but may remain
despite poverty welcome.

SATE

I will sing my lust no longer,
as my mad cry for your daughters,
o men of varied lands,
has become a virtual lament,
renewing itself infrequently
from the fragrance of woman,
now accessible
in memory only.

PROFILE OF FAILURE

Weak and fragile
from base of throat
to line of hair,
features sagging,
all sour, grim, sad.
Eyes that never kindle in delight,
mouth downturned and snarling,
nose a sniveling intermission,
unwittingly become
an etching doomed to musty attics.
I see this face sometimes,
flaccid in the mornings,
trapped in my mirror.

STRIVING

The heart leaps up with hunger
from a dreary, inert sleep
that marks many days of waste
swiftly spent in sad neglect
of vital obligations,
until awakening stirs
the desire for achievement.

WEAK SPECIES

We cry like animals
whose superficial wounds
will bleed and hurt,
but be forgotten,
while ours will fester,
then turn rotten
and in our inner selves
we cringe and wail,
like defeated hunters
driven from a jungle trail.

MIGRATION

Dwell not by the cold hearth
if the desired warmth
has never arrived
and blue from cold-fingered gropings
ended in amputation,
leaving us on the camel, hope,
named in weakness
when we're forced to join
the column of refugees
seeking the promised land.

JOINED

This no-sleep time
spent in barbed desire
as I drowse on bed of lust,
hungering a woman's flesh.
She comes to me at midnight,
silent as her passion,
greeting me with greedy claws,
falling on my waiting heat
a relentless ocean tide
cleansing a dank beach.

IT COSTS TEN CENTS TO PEE

This unworthy bladder
of transmutation
from one liquid to another
never ticks or tocks
when near a handy spa
(oh shades of Baedaker,
a watering place).
But wait until
embarked somewhere
without convenience of a toilet,
then the sudden surge,
that hidden rush of celerity,
strongest when nothing is seen,
ready for public upheaval,
pressing the urgent hunt
for a way station.
So I stand by the roadside
desperate and strained,
sans monkey, sans cup, begging:
"Buddy can ya spare a dime?
That's all the public rest room costs."

COUCH POTATO

Sunday afternoon
and the armchair quarterback
sends his blocking back
down and out,
but doesn't pick up the blitz
from his irritated wife
and gets really smeared
in front of his TV.

CODA

I am an old man
creaking with years,
who bends and sways,
salting my road with tears.
My weary legs desire
nothing but warmth from the fire.
I see the last day's sigh
froth from the declining sun
in an almost purple sky.
I am passed beginnings
and through with toys,
too tired for mischief
that youth enjoys.

Poems from *Tremors* have appeared in: *Alba: A Journal of Short Poetry* (Ravenna Press), *Bibliophilic Wanderlust*, *Bright Lights Café* (Bright Light Multimedia), *Concise Delight*, *Drown In My Own Fears*, *Everyday Poets*, *Exact Change Only* (Exact Change Press), *Farmhouse Magazine*, *Fissure Magazine* (Shadow Archer Press), *Getting Something Read*, *Gutter Eloquence Magazine*, *Hanging Moss Journal*, *Hash Magazine*, *Heroin Love Songs* (Dead Beat Press), *Nazar Look*, *Oak Bend Review*, *Ocean Diamond*, *Pirene's Fountain*, *Pocket Change*, *Poetic Medicine*, *Sephyrus Press*, *Short Poem Magazine*, *Sparkbirght Magazine*, *The Centrifugal Eye*, *The Houston Literary Review*, *The Ides of March Journal*, *The Literary Burlesque*, *The Montucky Review*, *The Nefarious Ballerina*, *The Ofi Press Literary Magazine*, *The Vehicle*, *Unfeigned Coffee Fiend*, and *UnFold Magazine* (Folded Word).

ABOUT THE AUTHOR

Gary Beck has spent most of his adult life as a theater director, and as an art dealer when he couldn't make a living in theater. He has had numerous published works including the poetry collections *Days of Destruction, Expectations*, and *Dawn in Cities*, and the novels *Extreme Change, Flawed Connections*, and *Call to Valor*. Gary's original plays and translations of Moliere, Aristophanes, and Sophocles have been produced Off-Broadway in New York City, where he currently resides.

www.ingramcontent.com/pod-product-compliance
Lightning Source LLC
Chambersburg PA
CBHW051346040426
42453CB00007B/435